fakemaggy

IF YOU ARE READING THIS
I TRUST YOU

fakemaggy

3. Auflage 2022
© 2022 fakemaggy
Alle Rechte vorbehalten.
Illustrationen: James Gardiner Covergestaltung:
Sara Schwarz
Gesetzt aus der Roboto
Satz: Lena León Pellegrin
Herstellung und Verlag:
BoD – Books on Demand, Norderstedt
ISBN: 9783756275694

to everyone struggling to trust sometimes

january

03
january

maybe we all deserve someone
who thinks they don't deserve us

can you
freeze the time for me
to live this moment endlessly
can you write
a book for me
to make our story infinitely

can you
cry and laugh with me
run and walk
dance and talk
and hold my hand to be with me

we can
cause I believe
our love
is like
infinity

rain and storm outside my bed
like inside my head

I will love you
like the night
loves the moon
and the day
the sun

I need you
like a flower
the rain
and a human
the air

I will protect you
like the snow
protects our world
and a poet
his words

I love you
like a candle
its fire
and a painter
his color.

I told my therapist about you,
oh …
wait
nope I didn't
cause you ain't gonna be dangerous for my
mental health

I am afraid
you drive me to
the loss of hope
or the need
to go

I am afraid
the tears I cry
are about you
or the things
you do

I am afraid
I'll lose the good
while believing
in together

I am afraid
I'll never get
forever.

low
glow
show
doesn't matter
where I go

living may be about making memories
but I don't only want to make them
I want to live them

12
january

there is so much
and so little in my mind
too much
and nothing to do

living foggy and chaotic minutes
while seconds feel like days
and hours run away

heartbreaks
made my heart
crack
more often
than I wanted it

art flowed out
like water from a mountain

so
maybe
it was
meant to be
like that.

the bad things reach me
the good things don't

at the same time I'm now able
to see the beauty of my city
I call home

I am just
a girl
with a poetic mind
tattooed on her skin

a woman
with chaotic thoughts
taped onto paper

anxious fear
an artful heart
and a life
that fell apart.

I am just
a girl
trying to try
crying words
and speaking pain
fighting hard
to live again.

I wonder
if you wonder
I think
if you think

I'll water
a flower
I'll give you
my hand

I ask
if you are asking
I question
if you are questioning

I'll lighten
a candle
I'll take you
by your hand.

some people still don't realize they
have choices.
they can stay or they can go
be honest or lie
stop blaming your past
make decisions to grow

unexplainable pain
running through my vain
searching for a way
of how to stay

lost sadness
walking through my mind
trying to find
a way to make me blind

maybe a dream
is just this,
a dream.

a thought in your mind
a story to find
words which shine

some imagined hope
a city out of gold
and a reason to let go.

22
january

homesick for the world

how many times
do I have to fly
to realize
I am alive

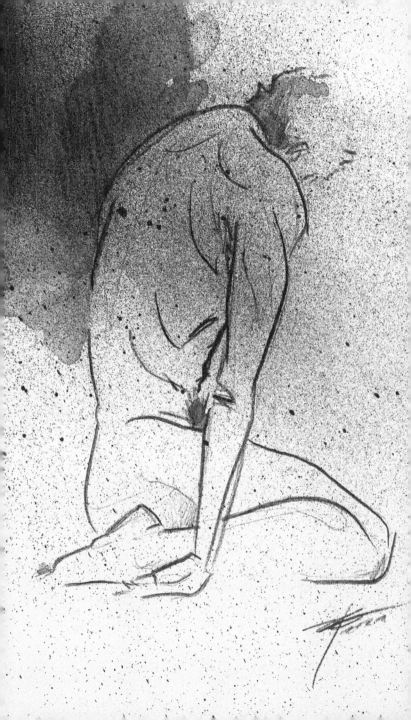

you are more than you think and stronger
than you'll imagine
better than your thoughts and bigger than
your worst

never had doubt
in my mind
anxiety in my body
and pain
in my brain

I had love for you
happiness and trust
lust of future
and the knowledge
of us

always remember how blessed you really are

time
will never stop for you
will never freeze
or care 'bout you

time is life
and life goes on
second by second
a new piece gone
like
everything and nothing
is going on

time and life
are running fast
but cheer you on
to keep it up
cause even though
they won't wait
they'll also never go away.

february

when you don't know
what to do
let it be you
who'll decide what to do

don't think
you are a fool

1
february

fog in your brain
it's all black again
nothing to see
feels like drowning
into a sea

trembling mind
nothing alright
chaos together
trying forever.

6
february

try and fail
cry but stay

feels like
everything is
a fight
an overgrow
a way to go

feels like
I do everything right
but the most things wrong
like an overstep
and a step back

like I'm way too old
maybe better alone
but loneliness
is my death

feels like I am right here
and somehow am able
to fight my fear.

dear alexa,
play everyone
who played with me
remind me of old times
and how they stayed with me
play me their songs
and sing out their lyrics

doomed to bake
a pie called life
which you need to eat
to stay alive.

some sweet sadness
half a cup of darkness
100 grams grief
mixed with disbelief

much furious fear
and dangerous doubt
with hopelessness
and much regret.

I found the me in you

it's difficult
and it may never be not difficult
cause you don't know
anything about the future
and know nothing
about how to decide
and what's right

it's not easy
it may never will be
but try
and do
fight
and lose

go for your thoughts
your wishes and dreams
go for yourself
to feel well
and go for
it all
cause you deserve to rise
after the fall.

I see the world
in words
I see it all
like poetry

I think
deep rhymes
and read my own mind

I paint
in letters
and sentences
notice it like messages

I breathe in lyrics
and feel in poems
my pain are writings
my joy are lines.

I see the world
in words
I live it all
like poetry.

23
february

love is a drug everyone is addicted to

It's a long
road
up the hill
a long walk
to take the pill

It's an endless
journey
a never ending story
something you can't hurry

It's a battle
against the pain
easy to throw away
but important to stay

It's a fight
against your mind
an arrangement of your past
a blurry of your heart

It's a long way
to reach the hill
but I promise you,
you will.

quiet storm
in an empty room
secret word
being said out loud
with a flower
which can't bloom
and a rainy cloud.

quiet thunder
in a crowded hall
important thought
hardly screamed out
with a day in fall
and a cup of doubt.

confused without a clue
nothing to do
a screaming mind
which makes me blind

lost in nothing
created something
a shouting brain
which brings me pain

I will never let you go
and I will ever try to show
to give you love
and help you grow.

you will never know the thoughts rushing
through the mind of others

march

opened book
so many pages
words of meaning
and some phrases

on page one
the look after
each other

page one hundred
what's life
you wondered

page one thousand
you've learned to love

page one million
it's time to go.

closed the book
no pages left
now it is
the time to live.

we are all so different
and unequal.
we are dissimilar
but even.
we are various
but the same.

as long as you aren't able to believe in
yourself
I will do it for you

take
your time
to heal.
to realize
and analyze
to love yourself
and give love back.
take
your time
to care.
to fight
and be alright
to protect yourself
and give protection back.
take your time
to be alive.
I'll give you time
to give you life.

wasted because of you
I wasted my time with you

I sometimes
write
instead of crying

live
instead of dying

I sometimes
create art
out of the pain

see it all
as a fun game

I sometimes
draw
instead of overthinking

and swim
instead of sinking

sometimes
I believe
in everything
won't leave,
keep promising.

finding yourself
is not about wandering around
trying to spot the perfect you.
it's not about changing your behavior
to fit into society.
it never is about acting
just to please others.
finding yourself
is not about walking around
trying to find the real you.

it's about listening to yourself
about observing
and noticing
it's about reading your own thoughts
about recognizing your feelings
and getting aware of how they are.
it's about breathing your brain in
to let your soul out.
about getting to know
yourself better and better
day by day.
it's about accepting
growing
learning
and loving.
it's about a journey
a walk through your soul
a travel through your mind
and finally about being fine.

every time you feel lonely remind yourself
of what you have
not what you left

let's go into quarantine together to get
some time together and talk forever

it's spring outside,
birds are singing
the sun brought a warm breeze
it's quiet outside,
nearly no cars nor people,
calm and peace are in the air
because covid told us
to stay inside.

listend to your words
tattooed them on my heart
made them art
they are my blood

watched you breathe
used this beat
created a song
listen to it on repeat

felt you go
painted your shadow
it's a while ago
it made me grow.

when I look
into your eyes
I only see
a reflection
of myself

when you look
into my eyes
you only see
a reflection
of yourself

does that mean
we only
see each other?

talk
without a sound
cry
with hope
laugh
with pain
lose
but win.

don't let the *what ifs* kill your inner soul

can you be
the reason
I feel loved
won't give up
and believe in love?

can you be
the reason
I get up
won't ever judge
and believe in trust?

can you be
the reason
I love myself
while you
will love yourself
so we can love
each other?

may the social distance
bring us mind proximity

shadows on skin
flickering
cause the wind
makes candlelight
dancing
while fingers
are drawing
imagined art
onto the place
where's your heart

it was the most difficult fight
in my life
to get myself
my freedom back

to go out into the streets
and not to stay at home and sleep

to walk outside passing by
without the need to cry

to get my comfort zone out of the house
and get it into the world

I fought
and won
my freedom back

but need to fight again
cause it feels like
I am trapped
at home again.

constant mood swings between it's gonna
be alright
and nothing makes sense anymore

you took the time
to paint the sky
to bring me back
to life

a cloud of pain
you made it rain
to wash it all away

countless stars
you drew them all
to brighten up the dark

you brought the fragile sunrise color
back after the day
to show that being fragile
is beautiful
and important
to be there every day.

instead of traveling the world
I'm traveling my mind
instead of hugging you
I won't leave you behind

instead of seeing a lot
I'm looking at my thoughts
and instead of touching you
I breathe in what you wrote

2020
and all my beautiful plans are fading away
like smoke in the wind
is my hope for today
but I will fight to be okay

home
never was a place
but a person,
a feeling,
and mixed memories.

it was.
cause slowly home got walls
thoughts
and I can let myself fall.

suddenly
it flew away
escaped,
erased,
didn't wait

suddenly
it hid somewhere,
vanished into air,
nightmare
couldn't take care

suddenly
the hope got lost
and left a loss
felt hopeless

so suddenly
you need to fight,
water your life
make hope grow
get stronger than ever,
find hope together
it will bloom forever.

I miss
your inspiration
our face to face communication

I miss
your hugs,
our laughs

I miss
your words
our talks
and how we are together

I miss
your company
us making memories,
simply having you
around me.

difficult breathing
heart hurting
skin shivering
mind racing
time is leaving

27|28
march

I dream too much
in the wrongest situations

walk that way
to heal yourself
fight that fight
to find your way

accept that fear
step over it
take your mind
throw love at it

never knew a certain way
try to stay
see myself fail

blurry view
shivering thought
the heart tears up
I fell apart
while my mind
is on a walk

trembling feelings
anxious fear
try to run
and try to clear

it will be
okay some day
I am here
to find my way?

I want to
hug your soul
and pick up the broken pieces,
puzzle them back
together
to show you
how to heal yourself
forever.

everything in my head
crawls out when in bed
gives me sleepless nights
with no power to fight

while it's quiet outside
someone is screaming in my mind
silence around me
means my soul is noisy

my body is weak
all I need is sleep
can someone please
stop my mind immediately

april

in my mind
we were perfect
together
close to forever

in real life
we were perfect
forever
but not together.

for some time
travel was an escape
a run away

a hide in better places
a story I created
but reality chases

and even though
I'm still not ready
to miss travel

I now will go
to satisfy and grow
to get new inspiration
love and interpretation
while I finally love
to stay at home.

you closed the book,
ended the story
but in my mind
there's more to read
and more to write
about our story.

show me around your world
all your streets
every little piece

explain how you think
how you lived
and all your dreams

paint me maps
to orient myself
I want to know
your inner self

inspire me
and make me think
tell me fear
and how you love

again and again and again
it's one of these days
where I'm losing again

again and again and again
depression is screaming
to love it again

again and again and again
there's too much pain
inside there in my brain

again and again and again
it feels like a game
but it's never the same

again and again and again
I'm asking myself
how long it will take
to fight this again.

silence makes me sad
with a mixture of peace

I can see them scream
it's a nightmare dream

I can hear them talk
every word takes a walk

I can feel them around
like every dark cloud

silence around me
reaches and hugs
silence surrounds me
like a human I love.

the wind told me
about you
and how much you miss me

I told the breeze
to kiss you
from me

the storm
whispered
our lovestory
to me

thunder screamed
and hugged you
from me

inside the hurricane
my soul touched yours
swirling around
we now travel the world.

speak
to create
I said
talk
to explain
I learned

write
to release pain
I screamed
paint
to complain
I dreamed

breathe
to feel
I tried
live
to love
I cried.

anxiety is telling me
you judged
you laughed
you'll leave

everything I say
is going to change
inside your mind,
paints a wrong picture
in your head

anxiety is telling me
I'm not only wrong
but also never right
and there's no chance for me
to win the fight

but in between
those stories
I'm having no worries
cause I survived
those stories

sometimes
silence is more powerful
than volume

and says more
than words
can tell

sometimes
being wordless
is more expressive

and sometimes
it will help.

I wrote you
into existence
my words became your heart
sentences your blood

my letters became your thoughts
my stories shaped your mind

my poetry
became your skin
my phrases
are your chin

I wrote you
into existence
you breathe in
my mission.

it is dangerously easy
to dissolve
into thin air

to get your skin
invisible.

it is perilously simple
to dissappear
into nothing

to get your mind
unseen.

it is
too easy.

you are
as dark
as shadows
but can't exist
without the sun

as black
as the night
but can't be
without a day

as cold
as winter
but can't develop
without summer

and
as deep
as hate
but can't emerge
without my love.

life
colored your soul
in deep dark black

so I bought a brush
to give it
some color back

now
your soul is colored
in colorful red

it will
take time
it will
hurt
and
it will definitely
be difficult.

you will
get better,
you will
see

that
you will live
the way
you will be.

I want to
draw shadows
onto you

read books
out loud
to you

listen to music
watching a view
going to places
we never knew

I want to
draw love
onto your soul

write stories
telling the truth
being together
just us two.

you are welcome to see
how my mind
vomits poetry

and invited
to read
my soul garbage anxiety

cause
inspiring you
is my favorite thing to do

even though
I still don't know
how I'm able
to inspire you.

ashtray
in pieces
shattered down
at the ground
crashed with a
none exciting sound

cigarettes
scattered around
the ones
we last smoked
when we were together
are at the ground

enjoyed
smoked up
thrown away
old and tattered
like the dreams
we used to say.

the only thing
I reached for
was the truth

but the only thing
I catched
was stone cold emptiness

thought
you would catch me
while you never even
reached for me

I want you
to understand.
to catch my words
and keep them close

I want you
to love.
to take my thoughts
and enjoy them all

I want you
to be.
to realize yourself
and self - believe

maybe
to love yourself
is sometimes
like loving your family

you had no choice
but got them

they sometimes drive you crazy
make you hate them
while you know
you can forever
count on them

there's this strong
invisible connection
and no matter what
you'll always chose
to love them

I walked a thousand roads
countless miles
and many mountains

I fought a thousand lifes
endless days
and million minutes

I struggled a thousand times
breathless moments
and loved the bottom

but I've won
more often.

she paints her art
in city photography
looks at the sky
like you look
at me

she writes her words
in experience poetry
looks at the nature
like you love
me endlessly

she speaks her thoughts
in day anxiety
looks at life
like you left
me totally.

left alone
with nothing
nothing full of emptiness
with growing doubt,
you watered it.

left alone
while you took right
with everything
that you created
in my mind.

left alone
now I'm with pain
lost it all
but don't regret
cause even though
we were worth it.

your way of living
your way of life
the way you think
the way you talk
feels like
it is my personal art

your mind,
you being kind
is music
in my eye

your hand
in mine,
me having you
by my side,
us living this life

gives me paranoia
that you ain't be loyal

29
april

learned to fly
into the sky
spreading the wings
which are broken inside

learned to speak
my words out loud
wrote a book
you misunderstood

but after every pain I took
my life
finally feels good

when you look at me
you can see
the wings you healed
and all the other
repaired things

while I only see
a reflection of me,
a tired soul
filled with no hope

but I know
I will believe
the way you look at me
to turn your view
into something
I will now believe.

you don't have to be brave
to be allowed to cry

you don't have to be sad
to feel bad

you don't have to be alright
to smile

while you're depressed
you can laugh
when you laugh
you can be depressed

you don't have to act
to bless
and nothing
has to make sense
at the end

when cigarette smoke
turns into words
I miss the softness
of your skin

while dreaming of
you next to me
I lost the key
of touching
real reality

cause all I see
in all the dark
is the tiny lamp
above myself
in my basement

I'd create
new hope
for you
would paint
the sun
for you
will give
a smile
to you.

I'd build
new life
for you
would write
the world
for you
will give
my soul
to you.

I'd die
for you.

to flee
from rational
and logical
I'm losing myself
in the silence of books
to take the time
and dream my life away

to jump
into the pages
swim
in those phrases
go
to different places

then closing
the book
the stories will wait
until I need
another break
from my real happy love
and my loving content life.

may

pain
dropping down
falling out
of greyish clouds

fear
lightening up
cutting through
the blackish heaven

doubt
drumming loudly
crashing into
noisy silence

dear universe
could you please
look down at me
and create
another chance for me

another chance
where it's okay
to be as afraid
as I'm in love
with changes

and possible
to be able to treasure
the pressure

dear universe
please
look down at me
and help
to give me the strength
I need.

you said
you'd take me to paris
rent a room
with a view,
say I love you
under the moon.

you told me
everytime
you looked into my eyes
that everything you feel inside
is pride.

you whispered
into my ear
you'd only feel well
when you were laying
next to me

you texted me
that it's the end
so I went to paris
with my friends
and now tell myself
how proud I am.

some
are like the sun,
a flower
in the rain
a strawberry
in summer

others
are like a wave
a grain of sand,
a slave
in life,
a long lost piece
at the beach

and some
are like the wind,
like a breeze,
a non heard whisper,
like ice cold winter.

what if
I only dreamed
that we met
only dreamed
in my sleep.

what if
I never wake up
to live
my dream?

can we stop time
and be alright

throw pain away,
make everything okay?

can we heal the world,
forever stay

erase the hate,
love every day?

can we all help together
to be strong forever?

don't ever
try to close your eyes,
to avoid insanity

or shut your ears
in front of me

don't ever
try to run away
from real life reality

or hold your breath
to influence me.

please accept
and if you ever
need to try the never
than
talk to me.

someone
will always
throw a stone at you

some on purpose,
others on accident

you will always
need to catch or jump,
to not get hit
by the brick

but there will always
also be
another person
who can not only see
but will also help
to survive the kick

and maybe
at the end
you'll get a kiss.

and even
if the day will end
and after we
will go to sleep
I will forever
give you the strength
you need to fight
all those loose ends.

unspoken words
are in your throat
crawling down
they won't come out

unrealized thoughts
are in your mind
sleeping like
there is no time

untouched feelings
under your skin
invisible like
there's nothing within

underrated
not recognized
when will the hidden truth
be brought to life?

you are more
than good enough.

more
than your anxiety
and thoughts
your dark moments
and your broken sanity.

you are more
than wonderful.

more
than your depressions
and wrong words
your despair
and hopeless questions.

you are much more
than you think
and more
that you believe.

when everyone
is suddenly
punished
to be the one
with a mask on

how can I
find the
real one
underneath?

I looked back into the future
and forward
into our past

vanished our story
and wrote
what will never last

I talked about tomorrow
like it is today
and I even promised
that I will try to stay

I hugged
your silhouette
and kissed
your non existence.

we will
grow old
and wise
together
share everything
and make our
kids
be friends
forever

we will
share our
stories
and moments
together
make new ones
forever

we will
write and talk
create
and make art
we will
be strong and fight
win and cry
cause when we are together
we will always
be fine.

we might
be more alike
than we ever thought
and maybe
slightly different
at the same time.

I'm sorry
that I don't worry
but I'd be sorry
if I'd do

I'm happy
that I don't care
and I don't care
when you're happy

It might all
sound evil
but the devil
is you.

love
may be
like coffee to me
or the coffee
is my love

it is my reason
to wake up,
stand up
keep on going

the reason
to work on
chill out
keep on growing

it is
my next to me
the always near
my travel guide,
maybe
the love
of my life.

If you'd
look me in the eye
you'd sometimes
see me smile
while I cry

you'd
always
see me fight
while I am alive
some pain
while you're in paradise
and worry
way too early

and sometimes
sometimes you see
some frozen time
while I look you
in the eye
cause I stopped our life.

a flower
lost in a garden
full of grass

a cloud
lost in heaven
full of dust

a feeling
lost in nothing
full of us

isn't
life just basically
a try
to simply be

and while
we all
attempt
to be

we miss
to see
how life
could be.

completely
relaxed
fell back
got the good feelings
all back
believe
I feel
finally safety

when suddenly,
as always
it all
crashed down
like I'm used to it
now.

much to fear
much more to worry
makes my mind
go blurry

much to hope
but much more doubt
guess
I need to hurry

much to see
forgot to breathe
stopped the time
please help me fight
and make me smile.

are you
on your way
to make me smile
while I wait
for you and cry

are you
on your way
to stay?

you
and everything we do
are the best feelings
I know
my place to go
and the love
we'll show

maybe
made some wrong decisions
never did
regret a single one

afraid of tomorrow
the unknown future
got punched by yesterday
but learned
from that way

emptiness
inside my head
did meet
anxiety again

they danced together
in the rain
caused a puddle
of pain

24
may

can't we stop
to always look for love
cause we forgot
that all we got
is already enough.

pick me up
at lost and found
turn me around
and paint me new

pull me out
of dusty books
open me up
and take a look.

my life
is like the weather

sun after rain
rainbow with a thunderstorm
no clouds again
then snow.

my life
is a coincidence
not influenced
decided by chance

like Russian roulette,
a gambling game.

dancing reflections
of the golden sun
painting shadows
at the ground
I will always
look for fun

flying pictures
out of clouds
drawing angels
up at heaven
I will always
look for hope

sparkling stories
out of stars
writing lightness
in the night
I will always
try and fight.

opened the door
without a knock
stormed in
left me in shock

rearranged interior
like you wanted it to do
left me then
in chaos I didn't know

as you left
you closed the door
stormed out
my house broke down.

carried
over mountains
shipped
over the sea

experienced adventure
and never went away

ran
against a wall
walked
through it all

won so many fights
without saying goodbye.

that's
what your body
did to you
so tell me
why can't we love it
like it deserves to?

just wanted
to let you know,
that you
are wonderful.

29
may

sometimes you need to give up fighting for
others
to start the fight for yourself

30
may

after you gave me life
I received your lies
after you loved
you left

everytime
you're in my mind
I'm burning alive
screaming in pain
calling for help

drowning in doubt
crashing down
breathing out,

then
turn around
fight, live, love
without
a pause.

can't get you
outta my head
after you laid down
in my bed

is it
the imagination we love
or the truth they play for us

is it
the what if it could be
we love
or the words they created for me

is it
the idea of a future we love
or the today that we have

is it
or was it
and will it ever be?

june

like
a blind one
who sees
a paralyzed
who walks
a mute one
who talks

like
a dead one
who breathes
a heart
that beats
and soulmates
who meet

like
a chance
after the end
white
after black
a day
after sleep

that's how
succss
after depression
feels like.

nothing but
a cloud of pain
in my brain
sunshine of fear
rain of doubt
but thunder
brings hope

my love to you
is like
an old house
rotten
but not forgotten

once taken care of
now left alone
in a city of nothing

my love to you
is like
an artwork painting
hung up
in an empty gallery,
a long lost treasure
something I thought
is not only better
but forever.

lonely streets
no sound to see
my only friend
who is with me
are rainy thoughts
to set me free

could you please
not only be
but also see
what's going on
around me

can we please
not only try
but also realize
that we can be
alright

how often
can a heart
get broken
how much
can it still
get shattered down

how often
can we still
get hurt
and
how much strength
to heal ourselves

did you know
that sadly
even if you tried
to make everything alright
you chose the wrong way
to fight
so you destroyed
my life

clear up your mind
and forget about
what's bothering you inside
for some time

in every tear
I cry
there's a little story inside
in every rain
that drops
is a little word
I wrote
but didn't spoke
cause I was afraid
of the upcoming storm.

nothing
can be full
of too much
to reach

too much to see
and more than you'll feel

nothing
can be dark and wide
grey and white

nothing
can be not a thing
and everything at once.

instead of talking
you walk

away from
yourself

instead of finding
your way

you stay
at the place
where it's darkness
but dark
feels safe.

a mixture of silence
and a clear blue sky
gets quickly exchanged
with dark clouds
full of rain
that comes by

a combination of immobility,
no movement to see
gets quickly replaced
with some storm
in a tree

that's how my mind,
my body inside
suddenly and sometimes
really feels like.

my heart
asks for pleasure
for laughter
and love

my soul
thinks much bigger
than my eyes can see

my mind
is a chaos
a not stopping machine

my heart
asks for pleasure
my body
will flee.

sometimes
when I walk
around the city
the wind keeps talking to me
my steps
are telling stories
and the air
keeps showing worries

sometimes
when I look
up at the sky
the clouds keep raining on me
my eyes
get lost in the wide
and the sky
cries.

oh
I must be dreaming
about the life
I'm living
oh
it must have been a wish
an imagination
that I live.

oh
I guess
this is what I've been waiting for
oh the one
I fought for.

oh
if I'd only knew
what's gonna be waiting for me
to do
oh I believe
I'd love my life
much more.

they say
get yourself
some confidence
to be
self-confident

but how to do
is a secret
to you

they say
love yourself
to give yourself
some of the love back
and give you credit

but how to do
is a secret
to you

and while trying
it sometimes feels
like dying
but tell me why
does it have to feel
like dying?

with open arms
I'll wait for you
and help you to
get through
everything
that brings the pain to you

in pitch dark nights
when again
nothing feels alright
I tell everything
I want to tell you
to the moon
cause at least
he's always there
and listens too

leaves in the wind
like
the sound of the waves
steps at the ground

like
my heart skips a beat
music by a bird

like
a dream you heard
life all around

like
love is in town.

I'm sorry
but my mind
is not only blurry
but also wants me to
always run to you
to tell you
about the good and the better
the bad and even the weather

I'm sorry
but my mind
is scared to lose
and afraid to do
something crazy
while I speak to you

I'm sorry
but I won't say sorry
if my mind
says me
come, run to you.

above the rooftops
the sun in the back
a candle in a bottle
the fire paints us

wine in a glass
the skyline up front
stories out spoken
I guess this is my home

I'd look at you
even if I'm blind
I'd listen to you
even if I'm numb
I'd be with you
even if I can't

it took
some time
to realize
that it's a journey
to learn about yourself
to be okay.

you are like a book
I sometimes open
but then you close

a page
with many stories
but while I read
the words will go

you are sometimes
like the author
and sometimes just the reader
of your book

and often you forget
that I not only want to take a look
but also want to be there
inside of your book.

while
you're supposed to protect me
you destroy me
more and more
day by day

instead of watering a flower
you pick it
to watch it
while it dies

while
you're supposed to help me
you hurt me
I told you
why you're supposed to go away
but instead
you try to stay
so you destroy me
day by day

30
june

I will
forever
protect my environment
and everyone who's around me
with my heart and soul

I will
forever fight and love
will cry and hope
respect and cope
for and with them

I will
forever
put my heart into it all
share my art
speak up
and protect
to keep it all
instead of letting it fall.

july

sometimes
you forget
or simply throw the fact away

that every little thing
is more exhausting
while being mentally ill

and that's okay
just don't forget
to give yourself
a break.

I miss someone
I never met
and need someone
I can't forget

I want someone
I never had
and crave for someone
who will accept

while the sun
slowly goes to sleep
the mind stops to breathe
for a second

years ago
I tried to dream
a little dream
'bout how life should be

in between
I lost my hope
cause all I got
were nightmare dreams

and suddenly
when I look around
I see my dream
in real life now

life
is a full time decision
to make
with the loss of lifetime
while we try to figure out
how to choose the right one

reachable
but far away
always around
and never there

sometimes
people
change your life
and they don't even recognize

powerful
but fragile
forever known
and no one knows

sometimes
people change your life
and show you one direction

24
july

in-between my art
you can
find my heart

and in my thoughts
my soul
written down
in stone cold gold

cause your heart
got broken
too much
you are afraid
of not being enough
but don't forget
that you haven't given up

I wonder
how life would be
if I would have worn your shoes
today

how my thoughts
would look
my mind would think
my eyes
would see
my heart
would beat

I wonder
how life would be
if it wouldn't be my poetry

did you recognize
the not planned,
the non expected things
are often way more powerful
than the ones
you're looking for?

laughter
and cry
birthed ones
will die

summer
and snow
flowers
will glow

darkness
full of stars
will tell us
apart

living that life
is the task
we need to happily
survive

august

there always is a surprise
right around the corner
waiting for you
to crash into it

and sometimes
the chaos-result
is as beautiful
as the surprise.

you kinda
stole my heart
and took my breath away
you kinda
took my words
and stole my fear of losing it

09
august

a stab .
in my heart
like a pull
in my chest
a trembling word
like everything I forget

you'll see pain
in my art
like I'm bleeding the work
we all will get hurt
but we'll be ready for it

all I need
is to look at you
to feel like
it's gonna be okay
some day

if it's the last time
I'd see you
I'll be the one
that kisses you
I'd write a story
about you
to always remember
what we'll do

if it's the last time
I meet you
I'll be the one
that misses you
I'd paint a picture
just of you
to never forget
how I saw you.

I guess
I quickly crashed into
the love I feel for you

I know
I didn't search for you
but always wished
for everything
you do.

so now
I'll pray
that life will be
this good to us now too.

your hand in mine
your heart aside
I'm in your head
you are in mine

my thoughts gone wild
I tried to find
how to reduce
my pain inside

your soul in mine
your fear aside
I'm in your mind
you are in mine

my doubts went blind
I guess I find
the way to fight
to be by your side.

29
august

I found a lover
hidden in life
now that I got you
I'm out of my mind

He found a lover
I was a surprise
now that we got us
we are changing our lives

september

suddenly
everything I think about
is you and me
the beauty of chaos
in my head
and the feeling of home
I get

this
is more than a love letter to you
my tiny little dog
cause you are better than good
and we love you more
than anyone else ever would

this
is a call up to heaven
a scream up to you
a plane packed with cuddles
and a bird
bringing love

this
is a thank you
to every second
I got with you
a cry
cause I not only lost
but also had you.

this
baby
is pain and grief
sorrow
and never ending endless love.

and as she walked around
the sky
she never thought
she'd see him there

the one she dreamed about
without being allowed
cause she was afraid
of her own expected creation

the one she was searching for
without being on a hunt
cause she was afraid
to never find the one

the one
who brought her down to earth
the one who gives her endless life
the one who treats her
like she actually deserves.

I want you
to be a part of mine

a part
of my heart
you already got
without even me
giving you that

I want you
to be a part of my life

a part of some time
you already got
but for me
that time
is never enough

art and pain
are sometimes
just the same

you are expressing
what's inside your brain

throw it outside
don't feel it again

so while your mind
is frozen in art

you helped yourself
to not fall apart.

disappeared
and vanished
went away
and panicked

managed
to leave the planet
tried
to heal the damaged

19
september

with you
on a boat
through my favorite city
the wind
in our hands
life is our plan

with you
on the water
through my favorite laughter
the sun
in our heart
us two
never apart

I want everything
and nothing
at the same time
give me the world
and I'll be fine

I'm not yours
and you're not mine
but we share much time

october

in my mind
you will find
everything
I think about

thrown into confusion
build in a chaotic way
words stuffed together
some sentences are lost forever

in my mind
you can find
what anxiety is screaming
mixed with the cry of my depression
and the hope I got

let me be a star
at the endless sky
which sparkles at night
and sees others living their lives

let me be the sun
to bring warmth and joy
paint smiles and let plants grow

let me be the moon
alone in heaven
brightening up
what seemed so dark

let me be
the wind and sea
cause planet earth
is what we need.

I am afraid
of losing
the love you got for me
to lose
our connection,
only see your reflection

I am afraid
of not being enough
cause for you
I wanna be
the best version of me

I am afraid
that I am
the wrong person for you
and I'm afraid
our time will be
soon a memory
to you

you showed me the world
from another perspective
showed me around,
some different places

you showed me life
from another point of view
showed me around
like you are used to

you told me a story
and painted your mind
I felt your heart
and gave you my time

10
october

slow waves
dancing like the beat of my heart
crashing against the beach
like reality against the way I try to start

frozen sand
dripping out of your hand
a slow motion fall down
like life building new land

moving sun
shining down to earth
like your love makes me survive.

I recognize
I like someone
more than I should do
when I live my life
and keep to miss
to share it all with you.

I realize
I love someone
more than I should do
when I look around
and all I think
is ,where the fuck are you'

I know
I lost myself
in a picture about you
is after I
did recognize and realize
that all of this
is true.

write down
every second
of how I saw the world

paint 'round
every city
I visited with you

rhyme 'bout
every minute
I fought myself through

draw on
every word
I did exchange with you.

looking at yourself
with pure love
is a privilege
to keep fighting for

feeling truly proud
is a case
to dream about

having no doubt
is a thing
for reaching out

looking at yourself
is something
we should learn about.

fear up in the clouds
raindrops
falling down
crashing at the ground
my mind is being loud

life down to earth
flowers
growing out
shattering the ground
my soul is getting loud

pain in the air
birds
flying around
racing against the ground
my head is so loud.

you show me
what I missed
and why it didn't work
with all the other boys

we are not perfect
but we will work on it
and use the time
we have.

I wish you can see yourself
through my eyes
so I write

I write about
your eyes
how they sparkle at night
the way you look around
and find closure
at the ground

I write about
your mind
what's going on inside,
the words that you can find

I write about
your dreams
the way you look at life

I write about
you and how you act
how you care
and keep to share

I write about
your love
and how you won't
give up.

life is different
to everyone
different
everywhere
and similar
in some way

life is the only one
we got
a chance to take
and the reason to live

life is love
and hate and cry
life is fight
and do alright.

22
october

a simple look
of your eyes into mine
make me feel
like suddenly
everything is fine

it's okay
to search for love
and to fight
to keep it
right?

nothing
sometimes
brings the darkest days

after endless joy
comes pain

and love
develops into hate.

everything
sometimes
brings the darkest days

laughter
turns into doubt

and trust
gets lost in hope.

november

too good to be true
is the time
I got with you.

when your mind
talks shit to you
let it talk
but know what's true.

instead of constantly thinking
about me
possibly losing you
I should hold on
to the wonderful truth

life is definitely everything
but easy

and easy
is a secret of life

06
november

words out of love
dripping out of my tongue
slipping down
to get to your heart

how much time
is left
for you and I
to get life back

how much us
is left
for us
to still have luck

how long
do we need to try
to get to the point
where the world
is alright

while you see peace
I see the hate
after another day
it's like a change

when you see hate
I found my peace
depends on how
you look at it

the world
and we
aren't black and white
so take your love
and share it right

maybe the
'I would do everything for you'
is the way
I lose

isn't time
and love
the only thing
we really have

so shouldn't we
start
to use it right?

instead of forgetting
we should take time
to remember
that we survived

read those lines
and feel alright
fight for life
and smile

rhyme about
your inner mind
process pain
and talk about
your inner thought

even if all seems so dark
somewhere around
you'll find your heart

the clouds get dark
the night rises
my mind is loud
I'm slowly falling
into greyish fall

the candle sparks
a time of joy
painting shadows
at the wall

the inside is cold
but in my soul
I still
am able to find hope

13
november

you clean my mind
you tidy up
you took my chaos
please never stop

you went away
and took my mind
what's left is chaos
in my head.

he saw her chaos
and went through it
he understood
what's under it

he was afraid
to never stop
he went away
and left her love

inside his mind
he tidied up
he fixed his chaos
got over it

love can heal
and destroy

be there
and go

stay
and fade
and even
is able
to turn into hate

it feels like
you took my words
and feelings
when you left
and the only thing that's left
is the feeling
that I need to leave
the love I lost

I not only miss our past
but already miss the time
we won't have again

I can guarantee
you nothing
but I'll keep
on trying
'cause the one thing I know
is that love
isn't dying

hope
is imprisoned
joy visits

winning
is hidden
power is vision

the time you write
is yours to fight
free the hope
and live your life

life is fast
my mind is slow
I'm still with you
while you
did go.

every loss
will bring a chance
every night
will have a light

being vulnerable
isn't only pain
but also being strong
to try again

I get naked all the time
not with clothes,
but with sharing
thoughts of mine

every win
an ended fight
every day
a story
you write.

29
november

oh life
I sometimes wish
you'd give luck
away for free

to let us see
how love can be
and treat
ourselves
to set us free.

december

never ending falling snow
seems like my way
of letting go

decorated town
with white powder
like my soul

we should always try to show
what's our way
of falling snow.

01
december

thoughts
drawn in black
blurry mind
comes back
– panic attack –
it's grey
in my head

hide me
in a world of color
throw at me some treats
hug me like non other
sing a bonus track
for me

a present a day
like a dream
that stays
the sky is grey

please be present
not only give presents
be my dream
instead of making me dream
stay
cause without you
everything is grey.

found over
in lover
and end
in friend

still never afraid
of having an end
cause I'll do it
all over again

you are my wood stove
in the living room
hugging me with warmth
instead making me freeze

you are my candle
in the night
painting shadows
and art light

you are the glass of wine
I got to hold
treating myself right

you are my wonderful
with all I ever need

highway traffic
in my head
cars are driving
back and back
rainy weather
stone cold snow
meets tornados
let me go

05
december

down
the ground
show
me snow
get me cold
and make me warm

up
the sky
see
me cry
make me wanna live,
not die

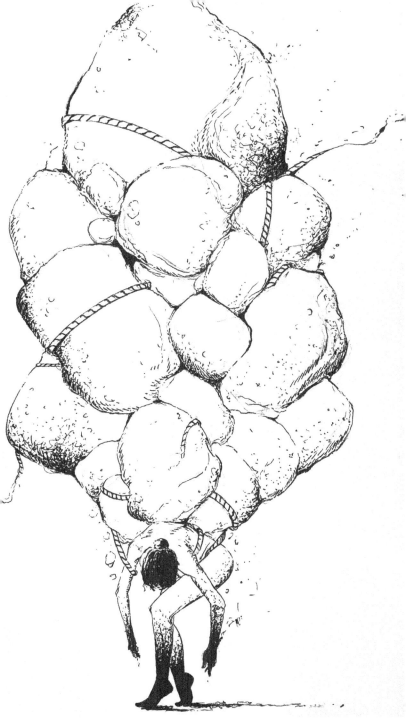

I cracked my heart open
thought I could find
pieces of you inside

all that I got
were drips of blood

alone together
to get
together
whenever
we'll do.

what if losing you
was the biggest mistake
that happened
and we did act
against our purpose

hold on
to life
even if sometimes
nothing feels alright

get yourself up
good luck
and fight

I believe in you
now please
start believing too.

when the tiniest
creature
is able to heal your pain
and throw negative thoughts away

you found one
of the miracles
our world
is able to create

today is a special and weird day for me
exactly three years ago today
I left my three month therapy at a mental
health clinic

I left with everything and nothing
with healed fear but panic
returned hope and doubt
courage but a lot of work

I left the best and worst time
to jump back into life
and to fight

I left without knowing where to go
what to do
and who to be

I left with
and without me
to leave
and find me

and I left
without ever having in my mind
that I'll be sitting there
three years later
with such a story to tell
of ups and downs
and the things I won

mental health clinic therapy
should be
treated as the thing it is:

a lifesaving horrible time
a fight back to life
and the start
to learn how to keep winning

she had
magic in her mind
let it free
some time
touched souls
and changed lives
from time to time

she had magic
in her mind

how do I deserve
is what you whispered first
I gave a kiss to you
and hid in it the truth

convincing
your mind
to believe what's right
is a fight

believing
healthy thoughts
is a search for life
and a struggle
to find
a way to win
against your depressed mind

my body
a study
of how to
find it lovely

lost orientation
everything the same
ran in a circle
tried to find the way

been there
done that
even lost the map

seems like
I forever run
around there in my head.

22
december

hope
ruins and heals
my broken heart

it hurts
to have the thoughts
of our life
inside my mind

and the knife
(called life)
that holds them back
to come alive

failure
is nothing
when family
treats you right

so choose
your love
and keep them alive.

thank you.